Goldwin Smith

Bay Leaves

Translations from the Latin Poets

Goldwin Smith

Bay Leaves
Translations from the Latin Poets

ISBN/EAN: 9783337778378

Printed in Europe, USA, Canada, Australia, Japan

Cover: Foto ©Thomas Meinert / pixelio.de

More available books at **www.hansebooks.com**

BAY LEAVES

TRANSLATIONS FROM THE LATIN POETS

BY

GOLDWIN SMITH, D.C.L.

New York
MACMILLAN AND CO.
AND LONDON
1893

PREFACE.

THE translator of Latin poetry has the comfort of knowing that he is separated from his authors by no chasm of thought and sentiment, such as that which separates the translator from Homer, or even from Æschylus. The men are intellectually almost his contemporaries. Gibbon was right in thinking that no age would have suited him better than that of the Antonines, provided he had been, as he naturally took it for granted that he would, a wealthy gentleman and a philosophic Pagan, not a slave or a Christian. He and a cultivated Roman of that day, or of Cicero's day, would have thoroughly understood each other. Their views of life would have been pretty much the same, so would their religion, so would their mythology, for the literary men of the Georgian era had adopted the Pagan Pantheon, and Jupiter, Mars, Venus, and Diana were their divinities. Even the conventional worship of the Roman Emperor would have had something like a counterpart in the conventional reverence for "great George," and the political temperament of the philosophic Roman would have been in exact harmony with that of Hume and Gibbon. Horace Walpole might have heartily enjoyed a supper with Horatius Flaccus; he might even have supped well, though he would have politely passed the dormice. He and his host would have interchanged ideas with perfect ease. This affinity is largely due of course to the direct influence of classical education on the moderns; but it was also partly due, especially in the religious sphere, to a similarity in circumstances between the two epochs. Apart, therefore, from mere difficulties of construction or allusion, the translator may be sure that he knows what his author means. Lucretius is further removed from us than the poets of the Empire in forms of thought and in language as well as in date. But he is brought wonderfully near to our age by his Atomic and Epicurean philosophy and by the sentiment connected with it. Sometimes the likeness is startling.

The translations are free, and it is hardly possible that any but a free translation can be the semblance of an equivalent for the poetry of the original. A literal translation, as a rule, can only be a fetter-dance. The general thought, the tone, and choice expressions are all that a translator can usually hope to produce.

It can be hardly necessary to say anything about authors so well known. Familiar to all who would take up anything classical are Lucretius, the real didactic poet, who used his poetry as " honey on the rim " of the cup out of which a generation, distracted with mad ambition and civil war, was to drink the medicinal draught of the Epicurean philosophy, and be at once beguiled of its woes and set free from the dark thraldom of superstition; Catullus with his Byronian mixture of sensibility and depravity; Tibullus, famed in his day like Shenstone and Tickell, about their fair equivalent, and the offspring of the same fashion of dallying with verse; Propertius, whose crabbed style and sad addiction to frigid mythology are sometimes relieved by passages of wonderful tenderness and beauty; Ovid, whose marvellous facility, vivacity, and — to use the word in its eighteenth century sense — wit, too often misemployed, appear in all his works, and who, though he had no more feeling than Pope, shows in the epistle of Dido to Æneas that he could, like the writer of *Eloïsa to Abelard*, get up a fine tempest of literary passion; Horace, whom, for some occult reason, one loves the better the older one grows; Seneca, seeking under the Neronian Reign of Terror to make for himself an asylum of stoicism and suicide; Lucan, through whose early death, which left his work crude as well as incomplete, we have perhaps missed a great political epic, and who, in his best passages, rivals the writer of *Absalom and Achitophel*; Martial, the creator of the epigram, the mirror of the social habits of Imperial Rome, amidst whose heaps of rubbish and ordure are some better things and some pleasant pictures of Roman character and life; and the marvellous resurrection of Roman poetry in Claudian. A translator can only hope that he has not done great wrong to their shades.

Both Virgil and Juvenal are read in well-known translations; nor are passages so easily detached from the narrative of Virgil as from the philosophy of Lucretius.

CONTENTS.

LUCRETIUS.

DE RERUM NAT.   PAGE

  I. ll. 1–40. Opening Invocation to Venus 1
  I. ll. 62–101. A Defence of Free-thinking 2
  II. ll. 1–61. The Consolations of Science 4
  III. ll. 1–30. The Light of the Ancient World 6
  III. ll. 895–1094. Against the Fear of Death 8

CATULLUS.

CARM. III. On the Death of a Favourite Sparrow . . . 14
    IV. The Old Ship 15
    V. Love and Death 16
  XXXI. Once more at Home 16
  LXX. Woman's Inconstancy 17

TIBULLUS.

ELEG. I. i. Farewell to Ambition 18

PROPERTIUS.

		PAGE
ELEG. I. ii.	Beauty Unadorned	21
V. xi.	Epitaph on a Wife	22

OVID.

AMOR. I. ii.	The Triumph of Love	27
I. vi.	To the Porter of his Mistress's House	29
II. vi.	On the Death of a Parrot	32
III. ix.	An Elegy on the Death of Tibullus	34
HEROID. VII.	Dido to Æneas	37

HORACE.

OD. I.	v.	To Pyrrha	44
I.	xi.	Ignorance of the Future is Bliss	45
I.	xxiii.	To a Coy Girl	45
I.	xxxi.	The Poet's Prayer	46
I. xxxviii.		Simplicity	47
II.	vii.	Welcome to a Long Absent Friend	47
II.	ix.	To a Friend who had Lost his Love	49
II.	xv.	Against the Selfish Luxury of a Degenerate Age	50
II.	xvi.	Peace and Quiet	51
III.	v.	The Patriot Martyr	53
III.	vii.	To a Girl whose Lover was Absent at Sea	55
III.	ix.	The Reconciliation of Lovers	57

			PAGE
Od. III.	xiii.	The Spring of Bandusia	58
III.	xxi.	To a Cask of Wine	59
III.	xxix.	The Poet's Invitation to the Statesman	60
Epod. II.		A Rich Usurer's Dream of Rural Happiness	63

SENECA.

Thyestes.	ll. 344–403.	The Stoic Idea of Perfection	66

LUCAN.

Phars.

I.	ll. 119–182.	The Characters of Pompey and Cæsar	68
IX.	ll. 189–213.	Cato on the Death of Pompey	71
IX.	ll. 543–585.	Cato at the Temple of Ammon	72

MARTIAL.

Epigram.

I.	xiii.	On the Death of Arria and Petus	74
I.	xv.	The Fleeting Joys of Life	74
I.	xxxix.	The Perfect Friend	75
I.	lxxxix.	On the Death of a Young and Favourite Slave	76
I.	xciii.	On Two Old Roman Officers Buried Side by Side	76
II.	xi.	The Diner-out Disappointed	77
II.	lxviii.	A Revolt	77

EPIGRAM.   PAGE

III.   xxi.   On a Slave who had been Branded by his
                    Master 78
III.   xxxv., xli. On Two Works of Art 78
III.   lviii.   Roman Life in the Country 79
IV.   viii.   The Occupation of a Roman Day 81
IV.   xiii.   On a Friend's Wedding 82
V.   xx.   The True Business of Life 82
V.   xlii.   An Exhortation to Liberality 83
VIII.   xviii.   Literary Chivalry 84
VIII.   lxix.   The Reverse of the Last 84
X.   xxiv.   On His Own Birthday 85
X.   xlvii.   A Roman Gentleman's Idea of Happiness . 85
X.   l.   On the Untimely Death of a Famous Char-
                    ioteer 86
XII.   xxxiv.   Vicissitudes of Friendship 87

CLAUDIAN.

IN RUFIN. I. ll. 1–21. Providence Vindicated 88

LUCRETIUS.

DE RERUM NAT., I. 1-40.

Æneadum genetrix, hominum divomque voluptas —

OPENING INVOCATION TO VENUS.

GODDESS from whom descends the race of Rome,
   Venus, of heaven and earth supreme delight,
Hail thou that all beneath the starry dome —
   Lands rich with grain and seas with navies white —
Blessest and cherishest! Where thou dost come
   Enamelled earth decks her with posies bright
To meet thy advent; clouds and tempests flee
And joyous light smiles over land and sea.

Often as comes again the vernal hour
   And balmy gales of spring begin to blow,
Birds of the air first feel thy sovereign power
   And, stirred at heart, its genial influence show.
Next the wild herds the grassy champaign scour
   Drawn by thy charm and stem the river's flow:
In mountain, wood, field, sea, all things by grace
Of Venus love, and love preserves their race.

Mother of life and beauty that dost bring
    All things in order forth, thy aid I claim
When to our Memmius I essay to sing
    Of nature and the universal frame —
Memmius whom thy own hand has crowned the king
    Of all that charms or wins the meed of fame.
Grace thou my verse and while I sing bid cease
Fell war, and let the weary earth have peace.

This thou alone canst do, since thou alone
    Mars, battle's master, by thy spells canst bind;
Oft does the God of War love's cravings own
    Unquenchable, and on thy lap reclined,
His shapely neck back in his rapture thrown,
    His soul to thine through looks of passion joined,
Feed on thy beauty. Clasp him to thy breast,
Fill him with thy sweet self, and give us rest.

DE RERUM NAT., I. 62–101.

Humana ante oculos foede cum vita jaceret —

A DEFENCE OF FREE-THINKING.

PROSTRATE lay human life beneath the spell
    Of dark Religion lowering from the skies;
Nor was one found to break that thraldom fell
    Until a man of Greece dared lift his eyes,
One whom no vengeful thunderbolts could quell
    Nor wrath of gods. But on his high emprize,

Chafed to sublimer daring and intent,
To burst through Nature's portals forth he went.

Thus his undaunted spirit for mankind
    O'er Superstition's power the victory won;
Past the world's flaming walls his venturous mind
    Through the unmeasured universe pressed on;
Thence brought us word how Being is defined
    By bounds fast set which nothing may o'er-run.
So trampled under foot Religion lies
While Science soars victorious to the skies.

Nor deem it sin by Reason to be freed,
    Or think I lead thee an unholy way;
Rather to many a dark and bloody deed
    Religion hurries those who own her sway.
Was not Iphigenia doomed to bleed
    By the Greek chiefs, though first of men were they,
Staining the altar of the Trivian Maid
At Aulis where the fleet by winds was stayed?

Lo! on her tresses fair for bridal tire
    The sacrificial fillet they have bound;
Beside the altar weeping stands her sire:
    In all the crowd no tearless eye is found.
The priests make ready for their office dire,
    Yet pitying hide the knife. When gazing round
The Maiden sees her doom, her spirit dies,
Her limbs sink down, speechless on earth she lies.

The firstborn of his children she in vain
    Had brought the name of father to the king.
In arms upborne she goes, not by a train
    Of youths that the loud hymeneal sing
Around a happy bride in joyous strain
    Bearing her home, but a sad offering,
There to be slain by him who gave her birth.
Such evil hath Religion wrought on earth.

DE RERUM NAT., II. 1–61.

Suave, mari magno turbantibus æquora ventis —

THE CONSOLATIONS OF SCIENCE.

'TIS sweet, when tempests lash the tossing main,
    Another's perils from the shore to see;
Not that we draw delight from others' pain,
    But in their ills feel our security:
'Tis sweet to view ranged on the battle plain
    The warring hosts, ourselves from danger free:
But sweeter still to stand upon the tower
Reared in serener air by wisdom's power;

Thence to look down upon the wandering ways
    Of men that blindly seek to live aright,
See them waste sleepless nights and weary days,
    Sweat in ambition's press, that to the height
Of power and glory they themselves may raise.
    O minds misguided and devoid of light,

In what a coil, how darkling do ye spend
This lease of being that so soon must end!

Fools! What doth nature crave? A painless frame,
    Therewith a spirit void of care or fear.
Calm ease and true delight are but the same.
    What, if for thee no golden statues rear
The torch to light the midnight feast, nor flame
    The long-drawn palace courts with glittering gear,
Nor roofs of fretted gold with music ring,
Yet hast thou all things that true pleasure bring —

Pleasure like theirs that 'neath the spreading tree
    Beside the brook, on the soft greensward lie,
In kindly circle feasting cheerfully
    On simple dainties, while the sunny sky
Smiles on their sport and flowrets deck the lea,
    Bright summer over all. Will fevers fly
The limbs that toss on purple and brocade
Sooner than those on poor men's pallets laid?

And as to chase the body's ills away
    Wealth, birth, and kingly majesty are vain,
So is it with the mind's disease: array
    Thy mail-clad legions on the swarming plain,
Bid them deploy, wheel, charge in mimic fray,
    As though one soul moved all the mighty train,
With war's full pomp and circumstance: will all
Set free the mind to dreadful thoughts a thrall?

Crowd ocean with thy fleets, a thousand sail;
   Will thy armada banish from the breast
The fear of death? If then of no avail
   Are all these baubles, if the soul's unrest
Yields not to bristling spear or clashing mail,
   If haunting care climbs, an unbidden guest,
To power's most awful seat, and mocks his gown
Of gorgeous purple and his radiant crown,

Delay no longer reason's aid to try,
   Since reason's aid alone can mend our plight
That walk in darkness, and, like babes that cry
   With silly terror in the lonesome night
At their own fancy's bugbears, ofttimes fly,
   Mere grown-up children, bugbears of the light.
These shadows not the glittering shafts of day
Must chase, but Science with more sovran ray.

DE RERUM NAT., III. 1–30.

E tenebris tantis tam clarum extollere lumen—

THE LIGHT OF THE ANCIENT WORLD.

TO EPICURUS.

O THOU that in such darkness such a light
   Didst kindle, to man's ways a beacon fire!
Glory of Grecian land! To tread aright
   Where thou hast trod, this is my heart's desire.

To love, not rival, is my utmost flight;
  To rival thee what mortal can aspire?
Can swallows match with swans, or the weak feet
Of kids vie in the race with coursers fleet?

Father, discoverer, guide, we owe to Thee
  The golden precepts that shall ne'er grow old;
As bees sip honey on the flowery lea,
  Knowledge we sip of all the world doth hold.
Thy voice is heard: at once the shadows flee,
  The portals of the universe unfold,
And ranging through the void thy followers' eye
Sees Nature at her work in earth and sky.

Of Deity the secrets straight appear;
  The gods within their calm abode are seen;
Abodes which rains ne'er drench, which tempests drear
  Ne'er beat, nor chills the freezing winter keen.
But over-canopied with ether clear
  They ever smile with glorious light serene;
While Nature's self doth every want supply,
Nor pain, nor care those mansions come anigh:

But Hell and all its terrors vanish quite.
  Though nought is left behind our feet to hide
The abyss from view, Hell nowhere meets the sight:
  Into my bosom flows the mingled tide
Of shuddering awe and of divine delight
  To see thy genius which all truth descried
Thus Nature's inmost mysteries unseal
And all her ways in Heaven and Earth reveal.

De Rerum Nat., III. 894-1094.

Jam, jam non domus accipiet te laeta—

AGAINST THE FEAR OF DEATH.

"Thy home no more will welcome thee, nor wife
   And loving children run thy kiss to share,
And make thy heart o'erflow with joy. Now life
   And life's delights are gone without repair:
One day has reft all that with bliss was rife,
   And widowed all that hung upon thy care."
So say they ever, but forget to say
All cravings ended on that selfsame day.

Were but this truth upon their hearts impressed,
   Changed were their rede. "Thy troubles all are o'er,"
Then would they say, "This day hath brought thee rest,
   Thou sleepest well after thy travail sore,
While we, round thy pale corpse with heavy breast
   Gathering, with ceaseless tears thy loss deplore."
Sweet after toil is sleep, then wherefore sorrow
For him who sleeps and will not wake to-morrow?

So, at the festive board, as crowned with flowers
   And cup in hand they sit, the revellers cry:
"Drink, comrades, drink; a fleeting span is ours,
   Poor mortals that we are, of jollity;

Nor comes it back. Then seize the flying hours."
    Fools that they are of a fond fantasy!
Can senseless clay for the lost banquet crave,
Or the lips miss the wine-cup in the grave?

So, when the soul is drowned in slumber deep
    We feel no want, we reck not, hap what may,
We miss not our own selves, nor care of sleep
    The bond to break, though it should last for aye;
Albeit our spirits then their mansion keep
    And consciousness returns with dawn of day.
How then if sleep for nothing taketh thought
Shall death, that hath no wakening, care for aught?

What then if Nature find a voice and say
    To senseless mortals who their end bewail,
" If thou hast drunk of joyaunce in thy day
    Nor let thy goods, as through a leaky pail
Water runs off, slip unimproved away,
    Weakling, give over thy unmanly wail:
Rise from the feast of life a sated guest;
Thine hour has come, go, turn thee to thy rest!

" But if thy days have all been spent in vain
    And life is now a burden, why to waste
Add waste? Why not have done with toil and pain?
    Nought in my stores is left for thee to taste.
Though sense and limb should unimpaired remain,
    Though the whole race of men thou could'st outlast,
Nought else have I to give. Nay, though thy frame
Could deathless be, still all things are the same—"

Would not her plea be righteous? How much more,
    Should one far gone in years his doom bewail,
Justly would Nature say: "Dotard, give o'er
    Against the universal law to rail;
Years thou hast had enow, blessings good store,
    But thou hast let all pass without avail
Craving for untried joys, despising tried,
Till Death unlooked-for stands at thy bedside.

"Resign, then, that which suits not withered age
    And go, since go thou must, with a good grace."
Deserved were that reproach. Fool, dost thou rage
    Because thou must, like thy forbears, give place?
Old things make way for new on being's stage;
    Matter is needed to recruit the race;
Nor sinketh aught to the dark realm beneath,
Whereof they prate; but life is born of death

And, being born, must pass away like thee.
    So the long line of generations wends.
To none hath Nature granted life in fee,
    To each one in his turn a lease she lends.
Think, too, of the byegone eternity
    When thou wert not. That which is past portends
What is to come. Why should'st thou start or weep?
In sleep what pain? What pain in dreamless sleep?

And for those torments, whereof fables speak,
    On Earth they all have being, not in Hell.
Tityus here feeds the avenging vulture's beak
    Gnawed by the pangs of love or passion fell;

And the poor slave of superstition weak
   Is Tantalus, though not, as legends tell,
The ever-threatening rock, but empty dread
Of wrathful gods hangs o'er the victim's head.

Is not a Sisyphus before our eyes
   When, in fierce contest for the consul's state,
Ambition sweats and strains to grasp its prize
   And still is foiled by adverse power and hate?
To climb unresting and yet never rise,
   To strive for greatness yet be never great —
What is it but to heave uphill amain
The stone which still rolls headlong down again?

To feed yet not to satisfy the soul,
   To live yet never of life's joys to taste,
Though in their course the bounteous seasons roll
   With ever-varying round of blessings graced,
What is it but, like those sad Maids, the bowl
   To fill with water that still runs to waste?
Hell's fires, the Triple Hound, the Furies, all
Are shadows that the slavish soul enthrall.

But of the shadows earth the substance shows
   In vengeful pains that the wrongdoers feel,
In guilt that death or tortures undergoes
   By dungeon or by scourge, by fire or steel,
And when e'en these are lacking, by the throes
   Of conscience agonized that nought can heal,
With forecast dark of sharper pangs to come;
A Hell on earth he knows who meets such doom.

Say to thyself, unconscionable wight,
   Ancus is gone, a worthier far than thou,
And many a puissant lord from empire's height
   Death, that reveres no sceptre, hath brought low;
E'en him, that 'gainst the elements would fight
   And led his armies o'er the Ocean's flow.
Scipio, war's levin, that smote Carthage down
Is turned to clay as is the lowliest clown.

Founders of Arts, the Heliconian throng,
   Givers of beauty, sleep the common sleep.
Not his imperial diadem of song
   Could Homer's self from dissolution keep.
Democritus disdained life to prolong
   When drowsy age began his sense to steep;
E'en Epicurus, when his course was run,
Departed, though, as stars before the sun,

Pales every lesser light before his light,
   Quenched by that orb of intellect supreme.
And dost thou then presume, insensate wight,
   Whose very life is death, whose day a gleam,
'Neath which thou wanderest stumbling with affright
   As one that wanders in a troublous dream,
Ailing, but what thou ailest knowing not,
Thus to rebel against the common lot?

What ails them could men learn, and whence the weight
   That presses on each overburdened breast,
Their days they would not spend, early and late,
   Seeking relief through change and know no rest.

Heartsick the lord from his abode of state
　　Hurries, then hurries back. With jennets pressed
As though to save his burning house from doom,
Headlong he posts down to his country home;

But on the threshold, seized with weariness,
　　Yawns, and to heavy slumber lays him down,
Snatching a moment of forgetfulness;
　　Or headlong, as he came, posts back to town.
Thus each man flies but flying from distress
　　Escapes not, since the cause is still unknown.
Peace might be theirs were they but taught to see
That everlasting calm their lot will be.

O doting lust of life that us constrains
　　To fret and fume when peril we espy;
The end is surely fixed; delay nought gains
　　Except increase of sad satiety.
Nor can man take an hour, with all his pains,
　　From Death who reigns throughout eternity.
Though long thy term of being, not the less
For that will be thy term of nothingness.

CATULLUS.

Carm. III.

Lugete, O Veneres, Cupidinesque—

ON THE DEATH OF HIS MISTRESS'S FAVOURITE SPARROW.

LET mourning fill the realms of Love,
Wail men below and Powers above!
The joy of my beloved has fled,
The Sparrow of her heart is dead,
The Sparrow that she used to prize
As dearly as her own bright eyes.
As knows a girl her mother well,
So knew the pretty bird my belle,
And ever hopping, chirping round,
Far from her lap was never found.
Now wings it to that gloomy bourne
From which no travellers return.
Accurs'd be thou, infernal lair!
Devourer dark of all things fair,
The rarest bird to thee is gone;
Take thou once more my malison.
How swollen and red with weeping, see,
My fair one's eyes, and all through thee!

Carm. IV.

Phaselus ille, quem videtis, hospites—

A ONCE FAVOURITE BUT NOW WORN-OUT VESSEL AT ITS LAST ANCHORAGE.

THE barque thou seest lying here,
Stranger, was once without a peer;
Sailing or rowing, she could beat
All craft afloat, however fleet;
This Adria's beetling cliffs know well,
This sea-girt Cyclades can tell,
This oft have Rhodes, trade's glorious queen,
And Thracia's rugged headlands seen;
Thou, too, wild Pontus, in whose wood
A tall tree once each timber stood
And on Cytorus' leafy brow
Sighed in the wind-swept forest's sough.
City and land of box-wood fame,
Kinship with you this barque may claim;
It grew upon your mountain side;
First in your waves its oars it plied,
Then over many a raging sea
It bore its master gallantly,
Good upon either tack to sail,
Or run before the driving gale;
Nor paid it ever votive fee
To gods that save from wreck at sea.
Now its last voyage is o'er and here

It rests upon this quiet mere,
Devoted to the Brethren Twain
Who guide the wanderer o'er the main.

Carm. V.

Vivamus mea Lesbia, atque amemus.

LOVE AND DEATH.

WE will live, my love, and play,
    Let gray beards wag as wag they may;
Suns that set repair their light,
Our brief day has one long night.
Give me kisses, give a million,
Thousands, thousands more — a billion,
Then let us madly mix them, so
That we their sum may never know,
Nor envy cast an evil eye,
Because it is so monstrous high.

Carm. XXXI.

Peninsularum, Sirmio, insularumque ocelle —

ONCE MORE AT HOME.

SWEET spot, of all the jewels bright
    That glitter on old Neptune's brow,
Peninsula or island hight,
    The fairest, Sirmio, art thou.

O bliss beyond belief once more
   From wanderings long on land and sea,
From far Bithynia's unloved shore,
   Thus to return to peace and thee!

O hour of rapture, when the load,
   Cast from the wayworn traveller's breast,
He lays him, in the loved abode,
   Upon the well-known couch to rest!

Then Sirmio, on thy master smile,
   Who greets thee after many a day;
Bright be the face of lake and isle;
   Let all things in my home be gay!

Carm. LXX.

Nulli se dicit mulier mea nubere malle —

WOMAN'S INCONSTANCY.

MY lady swears, in all the world she will have none but me,
None other wed, whoe'er may woo, not though great Jove were he.
She swears, but what a woman swears when lovers bend the knee
Write we upon the shifting sand or on the flowing sea.

TIBULLUS.

Eleg. I. 1.

Divitias alius fulvo sibi congerat auro —

[The poet, in reduced circumstances, settles down to a country life with his Delia, declining the invitation of his friend and patron, M. Valerius Messala, to accompany him into Greece and take part in the campaign which ended in the Battle of Actium.]

LET him pile up his heaps of yellow gold,
And o'er broad acres proud dominion hold,
Who watch against near-camping foes will keep
Through painful hours, while trumpets break his sleep.
For me, to ease with poverty I turn
Contented, so my hearth may brightly burn.
To set in season due the tender vine
And the tall fruit-trees deftly plant, be mine.
Hope of the year! thy promise keep, and still
With must my vats, with grain my garners fill.
When without reverence passed I stock or stone
That wears the holy wreath in field or town?
Do not I to the farmer's god each Spring
The first fruits of my orchard duly bring?
Ceres, bright goddess, at thy temple gate,
Shall hang, cut from my farm, the crown of wheat;

While in my orchard, reaping-hook in hand,
To scare the birds the farmer's god shall stand.
Ye, too, my household gods, though wide no more
Is your domain, shall share my humble store.
Once from my noble herd a heifer bled,
But now the poor man's lamb must serve instead.
This at your shrine shall fall, while swains about
Shall "A good harvest and rich vintage" shout.
And now my poverty I almost love,
Nor more desire o'er land or sea to rove.
But 'neath the greenwood tree the heat to shun,
While at my feet the purling waters run.
Yet sometimes will I take in hand the hoe,
Or goad the oxen when the wain moves slow;
Nor will I shrink from bearing home the lamb
Or kid forsaken of its heedless dam.
Ye wolves and robbers, spare my little flock;
If steal ye must, steal from the rich man's stock.
Duly each year I purify the swain
And sprinkle milk, mild Pales, at thy fane.
Accept then, gods, what my poor board can spare,
Clean is the dish, albeit of earthenware.
All wares were earthen in the olden day;
Man's richest plate was then the primal clay.
Not to the well-stored garners of my sire,
Not to ancestral acres, I aspire;
Little I crave, so I can lay me down
To rest, not on war's couch, but on my own.
How sweet, while to my heart my partner dear
I press, the wind howling without to hear!

How sweet, when wintry storms the champaign sweep,
Lulled by the pattering rain, to sink to sleep!
Perish all gold and gems, rather than she
Should shed one tear at taking leave of me.
Messala, war to wage on land and wave,
And trophies home to bear, becomes the brave.
My lot is beauty's chain to wear, and wait,
A menial slave, at cruel beauty's gate.
Let others glory reap; Delia, with thee
To live inglorious is enough for me.
In my last hour to see thy face be mine;
O may my dying hand be clasped in thine!
When thou shalt see me stretched upon my bier
Thou wilt give many a kiss, shed many a tear.
Yes, thou wilt weep, beloved, when I am gone,
Thy heart is not of steel, is not of stone.
Nor, trust me, wilt thou from those obsequies
See youth or maiden come with tearless eyes.
Yet, Delia, in thy grief my spirit spare,
Mar not thy comely cheeks, thy tresses fair.
Meantime we live, and living let us prove,
Ere that fell Shadow comes, the joys of love.
Dull age creeps on; soon we no more shall play;
Lips cannot whisper love when heads are gray.
Now is the time for frolicsome amours,
The time to beat the watch and break the doors.
For such campaigns I am a warrior good;
Who covets wealth may buy it with his blood.
His be war's pomp. I, happy in my own,
On wealth and pinching want alike look down.

PROPERTIUS.

Eleg. I. ii.

Quid juvat ornato procedere, vita, capillo? —

BEAUTY UNADORNED.

DEAR girl, what boots it thus to dress thy hair,
   Or flaunt in silken garment rich and rare,
To reek of perfume from a foreign mart,
And pass thyself for other than thou art —
Thus Nature's gift of beauty to deface
And rob thy own fair form of half its grace?
Trust me, no skill can greater charms impart:
Love is a naked boy and scorns all art.
Bears not the sod unbidden blossoms rare?
The untrained ivy, is it not most fair?
Greenest the shrub on rocks untended grows,
Brightest the rill in unhewn channel flows.
The beach is with unpolished pebbles gay,
And birds untutored trill the sweetest lay.
Not thus the damsels of the golden age
Were wont the hearts of heroes to engage:
Their loveliness was to no jewels due,
But to such tints as once Apelles drew.
From vain coquettish arts they all were free,
Content to charm with simple modesty.

Less honour from my love I need not fear,
She is well dressed who to one heart is dear.
And thou art numbered with Apollo's choir;
On thee Calliope bestows her lyre,
And then, whose gifts of converse are so sweet?
The gifts of Venus and Minerva meet.
For these by me adored will ever be,
Then bid a long farewell to finery.

ELEG. V. XI.

Desine, Paulle, meum lacrimis urgere sepulcrum —

["Cornelia's Defence," as this poem is called, is an elegy on the death of Cornelia, a Roman matron of the highest rank, wife of Paullus Æmilius Lepidus, and daughter of Cornelius Scipio and Scribonia, a lady of the house of Libo. It is in the form of an oration supposed to be delivered by Cornelia in her own defence to the Judges of the Dead; but the plan is confused, and Cornelia addresses those she has left in the world above as much as the judges in the world below. It has been suggested that the elegy was intended to be inscribed on her tomb, which was, as it were, on the confines of the two worlds. The obscure and pedantic style of Propertius makes it difficult to read, much more to translate, him. But this poem, especially the latter part of it, is hardly equalled in the writings of the ancients as a tender expression of conjugal and maternal love. The liberty has been taken of slightly abridging the opening, and of leaving out four lines containing flattery of Augustus, which seemed to mar the sentiment, as well as a little of the frigid mythology of which Propertius is too fond.]

WEEP no more, Paullus, where thy wife is laid:
    At the dark gate thy prayer will beat in vain;
Once let the nether realm receive the shade,
    The adamantine bar turns not again.

Prayer may move Heaven, but, the sad river passed,
  The grave relentless gives not back its dead:
Such sentence spake the funeral trumpet's blast,
  As sank in funeral flames thy loved one's head.

No honours that on Paullus' consort wait,
  No pride of ancestry or storied bust,
Could save Cornelia from her cruel fate:
  Now one small hand may hold her grandeur's dust.

Shades of the Dead and sluggish fens that gloom
  Around Hell's murky shores my steps to bind,
Before my hour, but pure in soul, I come,
  Then let the Judge of all the Dead be kind.

Call the dread Court; let silence reign in Hell;
  Set for an hour the damned from torture free,
And still the Guardian Hound. If aught I tell
  But truth, fall Hell's worst penalty on me.

Is honour to a glorious lineage due?
  What my sires were, Afric and Spain proclaim.
Nor poor the blood I from my mother drew,
  For well may Libo's match with Scipio's name.

And when, my virgin vesture laid aside,
  They set the matron's wreath upon my head,
Thine, Paullus, I became, till death thy bride:
  "Wedded to one" shall on my tomb be read.

By Glory's shrine I swear, great Scipio's tomb,
    Where crownless Afric sits a captive maid,
By him that led the Macedonian home
    In chains and all his pride in ruin laid.

Never for me was bent the censor's law;
    Never by me wrong to your honour done;
Your scutcheon to Cornelia owes no flaw,
    To her your roll of worthy names owes one.

Nor failed my virtue; faithful still I stood,
    And stainless from the bridal to the bier.
No law I needed save my noble blood;
    The basely born are innocent through fear.

Judge strictly as ye will, within the bound
    Of Death's wide realm not one, matron or maid,
Howe'er renowned in story, will be found
    To shun communion with Cornelia's shade.

Not she, the maid of purity unstained,
    At touch of whose chaste hand Cybele moved,
When other hands in vain the cable strained;
    Not she, the virgin of the gods beloved,

For whom, when Vesta's sacred fire was lost,
    It from her votary's robe rekindled sprang.
And thou, dear mother, did thy child e'er cost
    Thee, save by her untimely fate, a pang?

Short was my span, yet children three I bore,
    And in their arms I drew my latest breath;
In these I live although my life is o'er;
    Their dear embraces took the sting from death.

Twice did my brother fill the curule chair,
    There sat he when I parted. Daughter, thou
Wast born a censor's child; be it thy care
    Like me, by wedded troth, his rule to show.

Husband to thee our pledges I consign,
    Still in my dust there lives a mother's heart;
Around one neck henceforth their arms must twine;
    Father and mother too henceforth thou art.

Kiss for thyself and then for her that's gone;
    Thy loving breast the whole dear burden bears;
Oft as for me thou weepest, weep alone,
    And ere thy children kiss thee dry thy tears.

Be it enough by night thy grief to pour,
    By night to commune with Cornelia's shade;
If to my likeness in thy secret bower
    Thou speakest, speak as though I answer made.

Should time bring on another wedding-day,
    And set a stepdame in your mother's place,
My children, let your looks no gloom betray;
    Kind ways and loving words will win her grace.

Nor speak too much of me ; the jealous ear
　　Of the new wife perchance offence may take.
But ah ! if my poor ashes are so dear
　　That he will live unwedded for my sake,

Learn, children, to forestall your sire's decline,
　　And let no lonesome thought come near his life ;
Add to your years what Fate has reft from mine ;
　　Blest in my children let him bless his wife.

Though brief my day, I have not lived in vain ;
　　Mourning for child of mine I never wore ;
When from my home went forth my funeral train
　　Not one was missing there of all I bore.

My cause is pleaded.　Now, ye mourners, rise
　　And witness bear till earth my meed decree ;
If worth may claim its guerdon in the skies,
　　My glorious ancestors may welcome me.

OVID.

Amor. I. ii.

Esse quid hoc dicam —

THE TRIUMPH OF LOVE.

[In this picture of the Triumph of Love we have a glimpse of the Ovid who inspired the mythological painters of the Renaissance.]

WHY is this bed the hardest ever pressed?
   Why are these bed-clothes tumbled with unrest?
Why have I lain the livelong night awake?
And why do all my bones with tossing ache?
What! can I be in love, yet know it not?
Has the sly god found some unguarded spot?
E'en so it is; I feel the subtle dart;
Once more the tyrant reigns in this poor heart.
Wert best to yield, or fan the flame by fight?
To yield were best: loads lightly borne are light.
Oft when we wave the torch we fan the fire,
Which, left at rest, would presently expire.
The patient ox, accustomed to the yoke,
Is less belaboured than the newly-broke;
To young and restive horses is applied
The biting curb, not to the charger tried.

Contend with love, more ruthless he will be
Than if you unresisting bend the knee.
Cupid, I own thy power; I quarter crave,
Stretch forth my suppliant hands and am thy slave.
Pardon and peace I beg, the war is done;
From the disarmed no laurels can be won.
Crown thee with myrtle, yoke thy mother's pair
Of doves, a car thy step-father will spare,
There shalt thou stand while all the people cheer,
Handling the reins, a graceful charioteer.
Damsels and youths behind the victor's car
Shall march in chains, the trophies of the war,
While I, thy latest prize, with wounds still green
And fetters newly forged, shall there be seen.
Good sense and modesty shall pinioned move
With every power that combats conquering Love.
Thou shalt be lord of all. Around, the crowd
With hands uplift shall "Triumph" shout aloud.
Fond flatteries, folly, madness, at thy side
Shall joyous pace, thy henchmen true and tried;
These, these are thy resistless soldiery,
Of these bereft a weakling thou wouldst be.
Clapping her hands thy mother shall look on
From heaven, and shower down roses on her son,
While, wings and locks bejewelled, thou dost fare,
A golden figure in a golden car.
E'en then, if I mistake not, will be felt
Thy fiery shafts, and many a wound be dealt.
Those shafts, e'en if thou bid'st them, cannot rest,
E'en as they passed they would inflame each breast.

O'er conquered India thus did Bacchus move
Though him the tiger drew, thee draws the dove.
Then, victor, waste no more thy might on me,
When of thy triumph I a part may be.
Look at thy kinsman Cæsar, mild as brave,
Who, conquering ever, conquers but to save.

Amor. I. vi.

Janitor (indignum) dura religate catena —

TO THE PORTER OF HIS MISTRESS'S HOUSE.

[The porter, it will be observed, is chained to his post, so that we have here a picture of slave life as well as of Roman lovers.]

PORTER, to chain thee thus was shame and sin;
   Turn that unfeeling hinge and let me in,
Leave but the door ajar, though it should be
The merest chink, 'twere wide enough for me.
Love's service has my substance so refined,
That laws of matter scarce my motions bind.
There was a time when spectres could affright,
And when I dared not go abroad at night;
But Cupid whispered in his mother's ear
(I heard him), "Thou too shalt be freed from fear."
I loved. At once my terrors all were o'er;
Nor ghost nor dagger could appal me more.
Thee only now I dread, cringe but to thee,
Thou only hast the thunderbolt for me.

See — that thou may'st unbolt this cruel door —
See how my tears in streams adown it pour,
Think of the day when thou was standing stript
And, but I prayed thy mistress, hadst been whipt.
The prayer that once availed to save thy skin
Shall it not now avail to let me in?
Then my good deed with a good deed requite,
Haste to unbolt the door, fast wanes the night.
So may'st thou some day from that chain be free
And eat no more the crust of slavery.
Ah! to a heart of stone I plead in vain;
Fast is the bolt and fast it will remain.
Porter, beleaguered cities need such ward,
But peace hath no besiegers, asks no guard.
Worse than a foe thou treat'st an amorous wight,
Then haste, unbolt the door, fast wanes the night.
No troops, no arms I bring to storm thy gate,
My mate is love, I have no other mate.
From love I no more, though I willed, could part,
Than from my limbs I could divorce my heart.
Love, and one cup of wine, and these poor flowers
Fall'n from a reveller's brow, are all my powers.
Whom would such enemies as these affright?
Haste to unbolt the door, fast wanes the night.
Hast thou no sense, does sleep with its dull ear,
Sleep, which love never knows, shut out my prayer?
Yet past thy guard to steal whene'er I tried
The setting stars found thine eyes open wide.
Perchance thy mistress rests in thy embrace;
Oh, if she does, would I were in thy place!

Thy chain with such a solace would be light.
Haste then, unbolt the door, fast wanes the night.
Am I deceived, or did the hinges creak,
And the door, turned, a welcome signal make?
Deceived I am; 'twas wind that shook the door,
And, blowing, far away my wishes bore.
Come, Boreas, for Orithyia's sake,
And with thy blast this odious barrier break.
Silent the city lies, and in its flight,
Letting the chill dews fall, fast wanes the night.
Haste, draw the bolt, or look for battery;
This torch to your proud mansion I'll apply.
Night, love, and wine no moderate thoughts suggest,
These banish fear, that shame, from every breast.
My words are spent: on thee, deaf as the post
Beside that door, all prayers and threats are lost;
Fitter in darksome dungeon to be laid
Than guard the portals of a lovely maid.
The dawn with frosty wheels comes on the while,
And chanticleer calls wretches to their toil.
Lie there, O wreath, from my sad temples torn,
Lie at this cruel gate till night is morn;
Thee, when my love at daybreak shall behold,
The tale of hours thus wasted will be told.
Dull soul that shut'st out love, whate'er thou art,
Receive a lover's curse ere I depart;
And ye, bolts, bars, posts of this graceless door,
A long farewell, ye'll see my face no more.

Amor. II. vi.

Psittacus, Eois imitatrix ales ab Indis—

ON THE DEATH OF A PARROT.

[The opening is, of course, a play on the ceremonies of a Roman funeral. The Paradise of Birds is the best part of the piece.]

DECEASED, a Parrot brought from farthest Ind :
All feathered friends the funeral please attend.
In pious grief each tender visage tear
With claws for hands, and rend your plumes for hair,
Beat with your wings your breasts, and let each throat
Wail like the funeral trumpet's doleful note.
Why, Philomel, bewail that ancient wrong?
Thracia's grim lord has been thy theme too long.
One matchless bird claims every thought. The tale
Of Itys slain is passing sad, but stale.
Hither, all tribes that sail the viewless air,
But thou, sweet turtle, first of all repair.
In perfect harmony your lives were past,
Your faith stood firm and rooted to the last.
Orestes, Pylades, illustrious pair,
Like you the Parrot and the turtle were.
Yet neither love so true nor hues so brave,
Nor such a gift of speech had power to save ;
Nor that my mistress loved the pretty prize :
Lost prince of birds, in death thy glory lies.

Thy glowing feathers mocked the emerald's rays,
Thy ruddy beak the Punic saffron's blaze.
No fowl could language ere so counterfeit
Or with such lisping grace the word repeat.
Untimely snatched! from quarrels thou wert free,
While others fought, peace still was dear to thee.
Quails in their battles pass a savage life,
Yet reach old age, full both of years and strife.
Spare was thy diet; for thy favourite feat,
Practised so oft, scarce left thee time to eat.
For food the nut, the drowsy poppy's seed,
For drink the stream supplied thy simple need.
The felon kite, the greedy vulture live,
The doleful daws foreboding storms survive,
The raven still croaks on, Minerva's hate,
And scarce nine weary ages bound its date;
But nature's marvel brought from other skies,
Image of human speech, the Parrot dies.
A cruel power first on the fairest preys,
The vile fill up the measure of their days.
Thersites lived Achilles' death to tell,
Lived Hector's brethren when the hero fell.
The seventh day came, the light of thy last sun,
Fate's empty distaff showed thy thread had run.
Still in death's grasp thou did'st essay to speak
And shape Corinna's name with failing beak.
In the blest realm beneath a hill is seen
A dusky grove, with grass forever green;
There — the belief to piety is dear —
Dwell sainted birds, while no ill fowl comes near.

In white-plumed innocence swans float around,
The matchless phœnix haunts the holy ground;
The peacock spreads his glories, and the dove,
Billing her mate, renews her earthly love.
There, our lost Parrot, welcomed in the bower,
Draws feathered tribes to marvel at his power.
A narrow tomb the little bones will hold;
And two brief lines the story will unfold:
" I pleased the fair. So much this stone doth tell;
What more? I talked and for a bird talked well."

Amor. III. ix.

Memnona si mater, mater ploravit Achillen —

[An elegy on the death of Ovid's poet-friend Tibullus. Two lines of frigid mythology have been left out. How could a man of Ovid's taste speak of Cupid as the brother of Æneas and make him attend in that character the pious Trojan's funeral? The two mistresses with their contest for priority of interest in the dead might have been advantageously omitted; but this is Roman. What ground of complaint Tibullus had against Gallus is a mystery.]

IF for Achilles, if for Memnon dead,
    A mother's tears by eyes divine were shed,
Goddess of Elegy, let fall thy hair,
As mourners wont, and come, our sorrows share.
Lo! turned to senseless clay Tibullus lies,
And with thy own sweet bard thy glory dies.
See Love, with torch extinguished, broken bow,
Quiver inverted, joins the train of woe.

Behold his grief, by drooping wings expressed,
How, with despairing hand he beats his breast;
How the quick sobs his heaving bosom tear;
How drop the tears on his dishevelled hair.
Not Venus' self was more distraught with pain
When by the boar her beauteous boy was slain.
They say we bards are Heaven's peculiar care,
A sacred race, and inspiration share.
But Death for sacred things shows scant respect
And lays his impious hands on Heaven's elect.
A Muse for mother, a celestial sire,
These saved not Orpheus, nor his magic lyre.
For him in grief his father's harp was strung,
And with his dirge the woodland echoes rung.
Great Homer, too, from whose deep fountain fed
The streams of song o'er poet souls are shed,
Sank to the shades when came the fatal hour;
Verse, verse alone, defies the insatiate Power.
The tale of Troy for ever will delight
And the weird web unwoven in the night.
So will your names, bright pair, immortal prove
Nemesis his last, Delia his earliest love.
But what avail your rites, your timbrels now,
Or your chaste nights? Has Isis heard your vow?
When cruel fate thus bears the good away,
Forgive me, gods, I almost cease to pray.
Be pious and you die: frequent the fanes,
Death drags you from the altar for your pains.
Dost thou, a poet, trust in lines that burn?
Lo! great Tibullus lies in yon small urn.

And fire, O sacred Son of Song, could feast
On that sweet home of poesy, thy breast!
The flames that such a sacrilege could dare
Would not the majesty of temples spare.
The Queen of Beauty turned her from the sight,
'Tis said that she let fall some tears of light.
Yet was it better so to end, than lie
In common earth beneath an alien sky.
At least thy mother closed thy eyes and paid
Affection's last sad offerings to the shade.
Thy sister, too, in mourning took her turn,
And bent with drooping tresses o'er thy urn;
Nor failed the two, once to thy heart so dear,
To stand together by their lover's bier.
Delia, as from thy corpse she parted, cried
O hadst thou still been mine, thou hadst not died.
Claim not, said Nemesis, the loss as thine,
Know that his dying hand was clasped in mine.
If aught is left but name or empty shade,
Tibullus rests in some Elysian glade,
Where, crowned with ivy, in their youthful bloom
To greet him, Calvus and Catullus come;
And Gallus, too (were friendship's wrong undone),
The poet-soldier who both laurels won.
Together there ye live, if life there be
In yonder realm, a sainted company.
Turn, then, Tibullus, to thy peaceful rest,
And may the earth lie light upon thy breast.

Heroid. VII.

Sic, ubi fata vocant, udis abjectus in herbis —

DIDO TO ÆNEAS.

[Dido writes to Æneas who had deserted her. The reader will remember that Æneas, Dido's faithless husband, being son of Venus, was brother of Cupid.]

THE stricken swan beside Mæander lies
  In the dank grass, sings her last song, and dies.
Think not I hope to move thee by my prayer —
That hope, all hope, has sunk in blank despair,
No, but when honour, virtue, fame are gone
'Twere a poor thrift to husband words alone.
And thou wilt go, and leave me here forlorn,
Thy faith, thy sails by the same breezes borne,
At once thy cable loosed and honour's band,
To seek, thou know'st not where, the Italian land.
The hopes of Carthage and her rising towers
Have then no charm, though thine with kingly powers.
Here is a city, where thou goest is none,
That land is yet to win; this land is won.
Suppose the haven gained, what friend will come
To bid thee call the stranger's coast thy home?
Once more thou must feign love, be false once more,
And find a Dido on the Italian shore.
Where wilt thou see another Carthage rise?
Where feast, as from this tower, a monarch's eyes?

Or, if thou dost, if Heaven propitious prove
To every prayer, where wilt thou find — my love?
I burn, as kindled sulphur wastes away,
As wastes the frankincense on festal day;
Æneas' form is ever in my sight;
Of him I think by day, I dream by night.
Ingrate he is, untouched by all my care,
And were I wise, to lose him were my prayer.
And yet no hate in me his guilt can move,
I curse his falsehood and more deeply love.
Spare, Venus, spare thy daughter! Cupid, wind
Thy witcheries round thy rebel brother's mind!
Alas! my thoughts on baseless fancies run;
Nought of that mother lingers in her son.
Of flinty rocks was born thy heart of stone,
Gnarled oaks, fierce beasts may claim thee for their own,
Or yon wild ocean, o'er which lies thy way —
See! how with rising waves it bids thee stay.
Go not! Thou cans't not go! The storm is kind!
Mark yon white breakers driven before the wind!
Let tempests give what fain I'd owe to thee
And right be done to love by wind and sea.
Too much, though just, it were that thou should'st fly
From me o'er angry floods and foundering die.
Too costly is thy hate, if loss of life
Seem a less evil than the hated wife.
Soon will the sea grow calm, winds cease to rave,
And Triton's steeds skim lightly o'er the wave.
Ah! would such change could o'er thy spirit come!
It will, if pity in thy heart finds room.

The perilous deep is not unknown to thee :
Thou oft hast tried — still can'st thou trust — the sea?
Weigh anchor e'en when ocean smiles — how rife
With ills and hardships is the seaman's life !
Nor think the main to broken faith is kind ;
There traitors oft their treason's guerdon find —
Love's traitors most ; for, as the story goes,
'Twas from the sea that Love's great parent rose.
Lost, I would save thee ; wronged, I seek thy good,
And snatch my foe from the o'erwhelming flood.
Live ; thou wilt suffer less by death than shame ;
Live, while I die, and bear a murderer's name.
What, if thy barque yield to the tempest's power,
(Avert it Heaven !) will be thy thoughts that hour?
Then to thy mind thy perjuries will come,
The Trojan's treachery and Dido's doom ;
Then, stained with blood, and with dishevelled hair,
Thy much wronged wife's sad spectre will appear ;
Then, conscience-struck, Heaven's justice thou wilt own
And think the lightnings hurled at thee alone.
Awhile to pity and the sea give way,
Thy safety, sure, is worth a short delay.
Think not of me, but of thy youthful son,
Enough that on thee rests the death of one.
Thy boy, thy household gods, compassion claim.
Shall waters whelm what has been snatched from flame ?
But ah ! no gods thou hast. Nor gods nor sire
By thee were rescued when Troy sank in fire.

'Twas falsehood every word; nor I the first
In trusting to thy well-coined stories curst.
Where is the mother of thy son, thy bride?
Deserted by her ruthless lord she died.
That tale my doting heart unwarned could hear.
Spare not! my folly merits all I bear.
Ten years o'er land and sea a wanderer driven —
O who can doubt thou art accurst of Heaven?
Thrown on my coast, I harboured thee; scarce heard
The outcast's name and kingly power conferred.
And would my bounty had but ended here,
Nor lavished on thee treasures yet more dear!
Woe worth that day, when, as the tempest broke,
We in a sheltering cavern refuge took.
I heard a cry; methought the wood-nymphs hailed
My bridal; 'twas my doom by Furies pealed.
Avenge, O Chastity, thy outraged name;
I to Sichæus bear a load of shame.
I keep his statue in a marble shrine
Where garlands green and fleecy fillets twine.
There four times have I heard the call to doom.
Four times himself has whispered, "Dido, come!"
I come, I come! Dread consort, thine I am,
Though still I dread to meet thee in my shame.
Forgive my fault; strong was the tempter's spell;
I fell, but through no weak delusion fell.
A goddess mother and a rescued sire
Seemed pledges of a love that would not tire.
Err if I must, my error was not mean.
Give him but truth, where will his peer be seen?

From birth to death in one unbroken flow
Of misery runs my life, a changeless woe.
Slain at the altar's side my husband lies,
His brother does the deed and grasps the prize.
I leave his ashes, leave my own loved home,
And chased by foes to unknown lands I roam;
Escape a brother's hate, an angry sea,
And buy a realm — to give, false wretch, to thee.
I found a city that with rising towers
And spreading walls offends the neighbouring powers.
Then wars arise and threat with loud alarms
My frail estate, weak gates, and scanty arms.
Suitors unnumbered next my peace assail,
Each fancying that his rival's claims prevail.
Bind, if thou wilt, and to Iarbas' gate
Send me, an offering to Gætulian hate.
A brother, too, I have, whose hand imbrued
With my lost lord's would lightly shed my blood.
No more those gods, those holy things, profane;
The hands that worship should be free from stain.
Thy gods might grieve to have escaped the flame
Doomed to receive thy ministry of shame.
What if, cast off, a mother I should be
And in this bosom bear a pledge of thee?
The child will share its mother's funeral pyre,
And yet unborn be murdered by its sire.
Fate links a guiltless to a guilty life,
Iulus' brother dies when dies thy wife.
Heaven bids thee go. Why did it bid thee come?
Why to no land but mine could Trojans roam?

And say, has not this Guiding Power of thine
Tost thee long years on the tempestuous brine?
Scarce Troy itself would all these pains repay,
If still it stood grand as in Hector's day.
Simois is known, but strange is Tiber's shore :
Thou art an alien still, thy wanderings o'er.
And life may fail e'er thou canst reach the coast
For ever near and yet for ever lost.
Leave mocking visions ; grasp my certain dower,
Pygmalion's treasures and imperial power.
A happier Ilium to our Carthage bring ;
Here find thy promised land, here reign a king.
Is war thy passion?   Does Iulus burn
From glorious fields in triumph to return?
Doubt not, a worthy foeman shall be found ;
The conqueror's pastimes in these realms abound.
But, by thy mother, by the shafts of might
Thy brother shoots, the gods that shared thy flight—
So may'st thou save the remnant of thy host,
And none the ten years' siege has spared be lost —
So for thy son may blessings never cease,
And thy loved father's ashes rest in peace —
Wreck not the house that gives itself to thee.
I love — no fault else can'st thou find in me.
I came from no detested Grecian land,
Nor did my kin against thy country stand.
Hat'st thou to call me wife?   I'll waive that name ;
Thine let her be and Dido fears no shame.
I know the waves that beat on Afric's coast,
The passage at set times is clear or lost.

When all is fair, set forth upon thy way,
Now stranded seaweed warns in port to stay.
Set me to watch; I'll be a trusty seer,
Nor, even if thou willest, keep thee here.
Thy comrades need repose, thy shattered fleet
But half-repaired is scarce seaworthy yet.
Much I have done for thee, may yet do more;
For my lost hopes a respite I implore,
While seas grow calm and love, while suffering trains
My spirit bravely to endure these pains.
Refuse the boon, at once with life I part;
Thou shalt not trample long on this poor heart.
Would, while I write, thou could'st the writer see:
The Trojan sword is resting on my knee;
Tears down my cheeks are coursing in a flood
And wet the blade; soon it will stream with blood.
Thy gift well suits my lot, and cheaply paid
Will be thy parting tribute to my shade;
Nor will thy weapon first my bosom wound;
Love's shaft has there already entrance found.
Anna, my sister, conscious of my shame,
My ashes soon will thy last office claim.
Grave not "Sichæus' wife" upon my tomb,
Yet briefly tell the story of my doom:
Let with my name Æneas' name be shown;
The cause, the sword was his; the hand my own.

HORACE.

Od. I. v.

Quis multa gracilis te puer in rosa—

TO PYRRHA.

WHAT slender youth, with perfumed locks,
　　In some sweet nook beneath the rocks,
Pyrrha, where clustering roses grow,
Bends to thy fatal beauty now?
For whom is now that golden hair
Wreathed in a band so simply fair?
How often will he weep to find
Thy pledges frail, Love's power unkind,
And start to see the tempest sweep
With angry blast the darkening deep,
Though, sunned by thy entrancing smile,
He fears no change, suspects no guile?
A sailor on bright summer seas,
He wots not of the fickle breeze.
For me — yon votive tablet scan;
It tells that I, a shipwrecked man,
Hung my dank weeds in Neptune's fane
And ne'er will tempt those seas again.

Od. I. xi.

Tu ne quæsieris, scire nefas, quem mihi, quem tibi—

IGNORANCE OF THE FUTURE IS BLISS.

DRAW not that curtain, lady mine;
    Seek no diviner's art
To read my destiny or thine —
    It is not wisdom's part.

Whether our years be many more,
    Or our last winter this,
Which breaks the waves on yonder shore —
    Our ignorance is bliss.

Then fill the wine-cup while you can,
    And let us banish sorrow;
Cut short thy hopes to suit thy span,
    And never trust to-morrow.

Od. I. xxiii.

Vitas hinnuleo me similis, Chloë —

TO A COY GIRL.

CHLOË, thou fliest me like a fawn
    That on some lonely upland lawn,
Seeking its dam, in winds and trees
Imaginary dangers sees.

Does Spring's fresh breeze the foliage shake
Or lizard rustle in the brake,
At once it quakes in heart and limb.
Yet I, sweet girl, no tiger grim,
No fierce Gætulian lion am.
Then, no more, fawn-like, seek thy dam,
But bury all thy fond alarms —
'Tis time thou should'st — in true love's arms.

Od. I. xxxi.

Quid dedicatum poscit Apollinem —

THE POET'S PRAYER.

WHEN bending at Apollo's shrine
  The Poet pours the hallowed wine,
What think ye is the Poet's prayer?
Not gorgeous India's treasures rare,
Not rich Sardinia's hoards of grain,
Not herds from hot Calabria's plain,
Not meadows such as thou dost lave,
Still Liris, with thy silent wave.
Let Fortune's favourite dress the vine
That yields Calenum's priceless wine;
The trader, blest of Heaven, whose sails
Have safely oft Atlantic gales
Weathered, from golden goblets drain
The costly draught his ventures gain.
Mine be the light poetic fare
That my own garden yields. My prayer,

Son of Latona, is no more
Than to enjoy my frugal store,
  Sound both in body and in mind;
  Nor, as old age steals on, to find
  My harp unstrung or friends unkind.

Od. I. xxxviii.

Persicos odi, puer, apparatus —

SIMPLICITY.

LEAVE costly wreaths for lordly brows:
  Of myrtle let my chaplet be;
Seek not for autumn's lingering rose;
  Twine but the myrtle, boy, for me.

Of all that blooms there's naught so fit
  For thee, my boy, that pour'st the wine;
For me, that quaff it as I sit
  O'erarched by this embowering vine.

Od. II. vii.

O sæpe mecum tempus in ultimum —

WELCOME TO A LONG ABSENT FRIEND.

THOU that so oft where Brutus led
  With me hast marched to do or die,
What god my long-lost friend hath sped
  Back to his home, his native sky?

How oft, our brows with garlands crowned,
    Together, comrade of my prime,
We've made the merry cup go round,
    And lent new wings to leaden Time!

Together, too, Philippi's flight
    We shared (my buckler basely left)
When Honour bit the dust and Might,
    That tower'd so high, to earth was cleft.

Me in a cloud Dan Mercury
    Bore trembling off from war's alarms;
But thee once more the surges high
    Swept down the stormy tide of arms.

To Jove then be the offering paid,
    And here beneath my laurel-tree
Let thy war-wearied limbs be laid,
    Nor spare the cask long kept for thee.

Bid the bright goblet mantle high
    With wine, the sovereign balm for care;
Pour the rich scents — Ho! loiterers, fly
    And braid the chaplets for our hair.

Reach me the dice and let us see
    Who shall be master of our feast.
Mad as a Bacchanal I'd be,
    With thee, my long-lost friend, for guest.

HORACE.

Od. II. ix.

Non semper imbres nubibus hispidos —

TO A FRIEND WHO HAD LOST HIS LOVE.

THERE is a respite to the rain
    That mars the landscape, to the winds
That vex with ruffling blasts the main;
    A respite to the frost that binds

In its dull chain Armenia's hill;
    A respite to the storms that tear
Garganus' tossing oaks and fill
    With flying ash-leaves all the air.

But, Valgius, to thy plaintive cry
    For thy lost love is respite none,
Neither when stars come forth on high,
    Nor when they fly the rising sun.

Nestor's lost son was Nestor's joy,
    Yet the sire mourned not all his years,
And they who wept the Trojan boy,
    Well as they loved him, dried their tears.

Cease then, my friend, thy amorous plaint,
    And turn we to a nobler theme;
Great Cæsar's trophies let us chant
    And sing how Scythia's icy stream

And Media's river, conquered, roll
   In humble guise their shrunken tide,
While, bounded now by stern control,
   The wild Gelonian horsemen ride.

Od. II. xv.

Jam pauca aratro jugera—

AGAINST THE SELFISH LUXURY OF A DEGENERATE AGE.

THE palace soon will oust the plough,
   Our ponds the Lucrine lake outgrow,
Patrician planes in barren line
Supplant the elm that bore the vine.
Now violet beds and myrtle bowers
And the whole tribe of perfumed flowers
Scatter their sweets where olives bore
Their fruit to fill the yeoman's store,
While with its leafy screen the bay
Shuts out the summer's burning ray.
Not this the faith our Founder held,
That Cato taught and bearded eld.
The private fortunes then were small,
The Commonwealth was all in all.
Then no unmeasured colonnade
Rose one rich idler's walk to shade;

Of casual turf each built his home,
Such was the rule in nobler Rome;
While all combined with stately stone
To deck the temple and the town.

Od. II. xvi.

Otium divos rogat—

PEACE AND QUIET.

FOR ease the weary seaman prays
    On the wild ocean, tempest tost,
When guiding stars withhold their rays,
    When pales the moon in cloud-wrack lost.

For ease the Median archers sigh,
    For ease the Thracian warrior bold;
But ease, my friend, nor gems can buy,
    Nor purple robes, nor mighty gold.

No lacquey train, no consul's guard
    Can keep the spectral crowd aloof
That throngs the troubled mind, or ward
    The cares that haunt the gilded roof.

Upon a frugal board to see
    The old paternal silver shine;
Light sleep from care and canker free —
    This happy, lowly lot be mine.

The mortal frames a mighty plan,
    And framing dies, a fretful elf;
He posts, unresting, through his span,
    And flies, but ne'er escapes himself.

Care sits upon the swelling sail,
    Care mounts the warrior's barbèd steed;
The bounding stag, the driving gale,
    Are laggards to her deadly speed.

Come weal, we'll joy while joy we may,
    And let the future veil the rest;
Come woe, we'll smile its gloom away,
    Since naught that is is always blest.

Achilles died before his hour,
    Tithonus lived while time grew old;
The self-same boon the self-same power,
    To me may give, from thee withhold.

Around thy dome unnumbered stray
    The flocks; Sicilian heifers low,
Coursers of glorious lineage neigh;
    Thy robes with Afric's purple glow.

A home that fits a poet's state,
    A spark, though small, of poet's fire,
A poet's heart to scorn dull hate —
    All this I have, nor more desire.

Od. III. v.

Cælo tonantem credidimus Jovem —

[The desire for ransoming the soldiers of Crassus who had been taken prisoners by the Parthians is rebuked by an appeal to the example of Regulus.]

JOVE, so faith holds, in thunder reigns above;
    Augustus is a present god below;
His deity the conquered Persians prove
    And Britons taught before our might to bow.

Rome, could thy soldier, once by Crassus led,
    Put off his fealty, renounce thy name,
In a strange land a vile barbarian wed
    And drag in her embrace an age of shame?

Could the stout Marsian, the Apulian brave,
    Forget the shrines, the glories of his home,
To live in Median garb a Median's slave,
    While yet Jove's temple stood, while yet stood Rome?

This, Regulus, thy patriot soul foresaw —
    And hence did thou denounce the compact base,
Lest one ignoble precedent should draw
    In time to come dishonour on the race.

Sternly he bade let die the captive bands
    Unransomed. "Shameful sights," the hero said —
" Arms wrested from a living Roman's hands,
    Our standards in the foeman's fanes displayed —

"These eyes have seen — a freeman's name belied
 By freemen who the conqueror's fetters wore,
The Carthaginian's gates thrown open wide,
 And fields our war had wasted tilled once more.

"Think ye the coward, ransomed, will be brave?
 Ye do but lose your gold and honour too.
Wool that has drunk the dye 'twere vain to lave;
 Never will it regain its native hue.

"So genuine valour, let it once depart
 From its degraded seat, returns no more.
What, have ye e'er beheld the timorous hart,
 Loosed from the tangling toils, the huntsman gore?

"Then will ye see the slave, fresh manhood donned,
 On other fields make Punic squadrons fly —
Him who has felt the ignominious bond
 Upon his caitiff limbs and feared to die!

"Dreaming of peace in war, his craven heart
 Discerned not whence alone true life could come.
O day of shame! Carthage, how great thou art,
 Exalted on the ruined pride of Rome!"

'Tis said that from his children pressing round,
 And the fond wife that for his kisses sued,
He, as an outlaw, turned, and on the ground
 Bending his gaze, stern and relentless stood,

Until his voice had fixed the wavering State
  In counsel never given but on that day;
Then, through the weeping concourse, from the gate
  To glorious banishment he took his way.

Full well the patriot knew what torturing pain
  He soon must suffer from the foeman's wrath;
Yet did he move kinsmen and crowds, that fain
  Had barred his way at parting, from his path,

With mien as calm as if, the weary round
  Of business run and the long lawsuit o'er,
He for his green Venafran fields were bound
  Or old Tarentum's legendary shore.

Od. III. vii.

Quid fles, Asterie —

TO A GIRL WHOSE LOVER WAS ABSENT AT SEA.

SPRING gales will waft him back to thee,
  Asterie — wherefore pine?
With goodly bales from o'er the sea —
  Thy Gyges, ever thine.

Driven by the wild autumnal gales,
  To some far northern cove,
The weary night he wakes and wails
  For thee, his absent love.

Though from a lovesick northern dame
   An envoy steals, to tell
That Chloë's heart hath caught thy flame,
   And plies each potent spell.

Whispering how, as the legends say,
   Too chaste Bellerophon
By her, whose love he cast away,
   To death was well-nigh done.

How Peleus, too, had all but rued
   Dearly his virtue cold:
Each tale that fires the wanton blood
   But all in vain are told.

As cliffs that billows beat in vain,
   So is he to her art;
But thou, fair girl — there dwells a swain
   Hard by — guard well thy heart!

Though 'mid the wondering ring, like him,
   The courser none can guide;
None with an arm so lusty swim
   Down yellow Tiber's tide.

At nightfall be thy lattice shut,
   Nor look down to the way,
When thou dost hear the plaintive flute,
   And say no yielding Nay.

Od. III. ix.

Donec gratus eram tibi—

THE RECONCILIATION OF LOVERS.

[This and the piece which follows have so high and so deserved a reputation as works of art that one almost shrinks from offering a translation. It has been necessary to take a liberty with the last line but two. *Levior cortice* literally rendered into English would spoil the effect. The poem is evidently a dialogue; but the critics pronounce it bad taste to prefix the names of the interlocutors, Horace and Lydia.]

WHILE thou wert true, while thou wert kind,
    Ere round that snowy neck of thine
A happier youth his arms had twined,
    No monarch's lot could match with mine.

While Lydia was thy only flame,
    Ere yet thy heart had learned to rove,
Not Roman Ilia's glorious name
    Could match with hers that owned thy love.

Sweet Chloë is my mistress now,
    Queen of the dance, the song, the lyre;
And O! to death I'd lightly go
    So fate would spare my heart's desire.

For Calais not in vain I sigh,
    His city's pride, his father's joy;
And O! a double death I'd die
    So death would spare my Thuriat boy.

What if the banished love return
  And link once more the broken chain?
What if I fair-haired Chloë spurn
  And welcome Lydia home again?

Though he were lovelier than a star,
  Inconstant thou as clouds that fly
And curst as Adria's waters are, —
  With thee I'd live, with thee I'd die.

OD. III. XIII.

O fons Bandusiæ, splendidior vitro —

THE SPRING OF BANDUSIA.

SPRING OF BANDUSIA, crystal clear,
  Worthy this cup of mantling wine,
These votive flowers which here I bear;
  To-morrow shall a kid be thine —

Yon kid whose horns begin to bud
  And tell of coming love and fight,
In vain; the little wanton's blood
  Is doomed to dye thy streamlet bright.

Midsummer's noon with scorching ray
  Taints not thy virgin wave, and dear
Is its cool draught at close of day
  To wandering flock and weary steer.

Thou too shalt be a spring renowned,
   If verse of mine can fame bestow
On yonder grot, with holm-oak crowned,
   From which thy babbling waters flow.

Od. III. xxi.

O nata mecum consule Manlio —

TO A CASK OF WINE MADE IN THE YEAR IN WHICH HORACE WAS BORN.

MY good contemporary cask, whatever thou dost keep
Stored up in thee — smiles, tears, wild loves, mad brawls, or easy sleep —
Whate'er thy grape was charged withal, thy hour is come; descend;
Corvinus bids; my mellowest wine must greet my dearest friend.
Sage and Socratic though he be, the juice he will not spurn,
That many a time made glow, they say, old Cato's virtue stern.
There's not a heart so hard but thou beneath its guard canst steal,
There's not a soul so close but thou its secret canst reveal.
There's no despair but thou canst cheer, no wretch's lot so low
But thou canst raise, and bid him brave the tyrant and the foe.

Please Bacchus and the Queen of Love and the
    linked Graces three,
Till lamps shall fail and stars grow pale, we'll make a
    night with thee.

Od. III. xxix.

Tyrrhena regum progenies —

THE POET'S INVITATION TO THE STATESMAN.

SCION of old Etruria's royal line,
    Mæcenas, all awaits thee in my home;
For thee is broached the cask of mellow wine,
    For thee the perfume breathes, the roses bloom.

Delay no more, but come, O long desired;
    Turn not thine eyes to Tiber's falling tide
And Æsula, on her rich slope retired,
    And yonder hill, hold of the Parricide.

Leave luxury, my friend, that only cloys
    And thy proud mansion's heavenward-soaring dome;
Bid for an hour farewell to smoke and noise
    And all that dazzles in imperial Rome.

Oft has a change been pleasing to the great,
    Oft the trim cottage and its simple fare
Served 'mid no purple tapestries of state,
    Have smoothed the wrinkles on the brow of care.

Andromeda's bright Sire now lights on high
   His cresset, Procyon darts his burning rays,
The Lion's star ridès rampant in the sky,
   And summer brings again the sultry days.

Now with their panting flocks the weary swains
   To cooling stream and bosky dell repair;
Along the lea deep noontide silence reigns,
   No breath is stirring in the noontide air.

Thou still art busied with a statesman's toils,
   Still labouring to forecast with patriot breast
Bactria's designs, Scythia's impending broils,
   The storms that gather in the distant East.

Heaven in its wisdom bids the future lie
   Wrapt in the darkness of profoundest night,
And smiles when anxious mortals strive to pry
   Beyond the limits fixed to mortal sight.

Serenely meet the present; all beside
   Is like yon stream that now along the plain
Floats towards the Tuscan sea with tranquil tide,
   Soon — when the deluge of downpouring rain

Stirs the calm waters to a wilder mood —
   Whirls down trees, flocks, and folds with angry swell,
While with the din loud roars the neighbouring wood,
   And echo shouts her answer from the fell.

The happy master of one cheerful soul
  Is he, who still can cry at close of day —
"Life has been mine! To-morrow let the pole
  Be dark with cloud or beam with genial ray,

"As Jove may will; but to reverse the past
  Or to annul, not Jove himself hath power;
Not Jove himself can uncreate or blast
  Joys once borne onward by the flying hour.

"Fortune exulting in her cruel trade,
  Sporting with hearts, mocking her victim's sighs,
Smiles on us all in turn, a fickle jade,
  Bestows on each in turn her fleeting prize.

"While she is mine, 'tis well; but if her wing
  She wave, with all her gifts I lightly part,
The mantle of my virtue round me fling,
  And clasp undowered honour to my heart.

"Blow winds, let mainmasts crack! No need have I
  To bribe the gods with vows or lift in prayer
My frantic hands, lest the rich argosy
  Freighted with Cyprian or with Tyrian ware

"Add to the treasures of the greedy main.
  Safe in my shallop while the tempests rave,
And, shielded by the Heavenly Brothers twain,
  I dare the hurly of the Ægean wave."

Epode II.

Beatus ille, qui procul negotiis —

A RICH USURER'S DREAM OF RURAL HAPPINESS.

"BLEST man who, far from care and strife,
    Leads like the men of yore his life,
Who tills his old paternal lot,
Whom grasping usury troubles not,
Whom trumpet never wakes from sleep,
Who quakes not at the angry deep,
Who shuns the courts, nor cares to wait
A suitor at the rich man's gate.
In wedlock now his task to join
The poplar tall and blooming vine,
And now to watch his kine that feed
And low in some sequestered mead;
To prune away the barren shoot
And graft the happier hope of fruit.
The honey in the cleanly crock
To store, or shear the panting flock.
When autumn in the fields, a queen
Crowned with her ruddy fruits is seen,
Blithely he plucks the grafted pear
Or purple grape, meet gifts to bear,
God of the garden, to thy shrine,
Or, God of Boundaries, to thine.
Now in the ancient holm-oak's shade,
Now on the matted greensward laid,

He takes his ease. The river's flow
Is heard, birds warble on the bough,
And trickling springs their music keep
To lull the soul to quiet sleep.
When winter with its blustering storms
Of rain and snow the scene transforms,
With hounds and toils and merry din
He hems the doughty wild boar in,
Or for the hungry thrushes sets
On slender sticks the viewless nets;
Or wandering geese and tim'rous hares,
Sweet morsels for his board, he snares.
Amidst such scenes as these what heart
Would not forget a lover's smart?
Give me a partner chaste and good
To keep my house and rear my brood
(Like those that graced the Sabine State,
Or lithe Apulian's sunburnt mate)
To make the fire more brightly burn
Against her tired goodman's return,
To pen the heavy-uddered kine
And fill the pails, to broach the wine —
Our last year's vintage, sound and sweet —
And furnish forth the unbought treat.
For Lucrine shell-fish naught I care,
Naught for the turbot or the scar,
Driven by the blustering winter's breeze
From Eastern to Italian seas.
No game in distant Afric sought
Or of Ionian fowlers bought

Would half so much my palate please
As olives from the goodliest trees,
The wholesome mallow and the blade
Of sorrel plucked in grassy glade,
Lamb sacrificed on festal day,
Or kid, the wolf's recovered prey.
How sweet, while thus we feast, to see
The sheep fast trooping from the lea,
The weary ox, slow-pacing, come
With the inverted plowshare home,
And slave boys, sleek and full of mirth,
Gathering around the blazing hearth."
    So said Old Ten-per-cent, when he
    A jolly farmer fain would be.
    His moneys he called in amain —
    Next week he put them out again.

SENECA.

THYESTES, 344-403.

Regem non faciunt opes —

THE STOIC IDEA OF PERFECTION.

WHAT makes the king? His treasure? No;
    Nor yet the circlet on his brow,
Nor yet the purple robe of state,
Nor yet the golden palace gate.
The king is he who knows not fear,
Whose breast no angry passions tear,
Who scorns insane ambition's wreath,
The maddening crowd's inconstant breath,
The wealth of Europe's mines, the gold
In the bright tide of Tagus rolled,
And the unmeasured stores of grain
Garnered from Libya's sultry plain,
Who quails not at the levin stroke,
On raging storms can calmly look,
Though the wild winds on Adria rave
And round him swells the threatening wave,
Who trembles not at thrust of spear,
Feels of the flashing steel no fear,

Who from his spirit's height serene
Looks down upon the troubled scene,
And, uncomplaining, when his date
Has come, goes forth to meet his fate.
With kings in grandeur let them vie
Before whose arms wild Dahans fly,
Who o'er Arabia's burning sea
Stretch out their gorgeous empery,
Who dare Sarmatian horsemen brave
And march o'er Danube's frozen wave
Or the strange land of fleecy trees.
True kingship is a mind at ease.
No need is there of charger's might,
Of Parthian arrow shot in flight;
Of engines dire, whose hurtling showers
Of missiles shake beleaguered towers.
The king, a king self-crowned, is he
Who from desire and fear is free.
Who would the power of courtiers share
May mount ambition's slippery stair;
To live by all the world forgot
In ease and quiet be my lot,
And as my noiseless days glide past
To rest unnoted to the last.
    Well may the man his end bemoan
    Who dies to others too well-known,
    A stranger to himself alone.

LUCAN.

Pharsalia I. 119-182.

[The opening of the Civil War. The reference in the first line is to Julia, daughter of Cæsar and wife of Pompey, whose death has been narrated.]

HER death the bond between the leaders broke
   And called to war; then rival passions woke.
That new achievements might o'er old prevail,
Piratic laurels before Gallic pale,
Was Pompey's fear. His rival in the race,
Now flushed with victory, scorned the second place.
Cæsar in power would no superior own,
Pompey would brook no partner of his throne.
Which of the chiefs had right upon his side
Is not for mortal judgment to decide,
Since either cause had warranty divine,
The winning Heaven's, the losing, Cato, thine.
Ill were the champions matched. One, agèd grown,
Had long exchanged the corselet for the gown;
In peace forgotten the commander's art,
And learned to play the politician's part,
To court the suffrage of the crowd, and hear
In his own Theatre the venal cheer.

Idly he rested on his ancient fame,
And was the shadow of a mighty name.
Like the huge oak which towers above the fields,
Decked with ancestral spoils and votive shields.
Its roots once mighty, loosened by decay,
Hold it no more; weight is its only stay;
Its naked limbs bespeak its glories past,
And by its trunk, not leaves, a shade is cast;
It totters to each breeze, yet in the ring
Of lusty greenwood stands alone a king.
Not such the talisman of Cæsar's name;
But Cæsar had, in place of empty fame,
The unresting soul, the resolution high
Which shuts out every thought but victory.
Whate'er his goal, nor mercy nor dismay
He owned, but drew the sword and cleft his way;
Pressed each advantage that his fortune gave;
Constrained the stars to combat for the brave;
Swept from his path whate'er his rise delayed,
And marched triumphant through the wreck he made.
So, while the crashing thunder peals on high,
Leaps the live lightning from the storm-rent sky,
Affrights the people with its dazzling flame,
Smites e'en his temple from whose hand it came,
Winged with destruction flashes to and fro,
O'erthrows to reach and reaches to o'erthrow.
Such private causes moved the chiefs; but Rome
Was drawn by empire's sins to empire's doom.
'Whelmed by the riches of the conquered earth
The virtue perished which gave greatness birth.

From boundless plunder boundless luxury grew,
The pomp of palaces no measure knew;
Old fare pleased pampered appetite no more;
Robes which had shamed a woman manhood wore.
Field unto field was added till the plain
Was turned to one luxurious lord's domain,
While herds of foreign slaves their fetters wore
Where Roman heroes held the plough of yore.
A peaceful happiness had lost its charms,
Mere freedom palled on hearts that craved for arms.
When passion bade, at once they drew the sword;
Crime was no crime when need had given the word.
With traitorous arms the country to enslave
Was deemed the crowning glory of the brave.
Now force made law, force turned the people's vote,
Force with its ruffian hand the statute wrote.
To duty lost, tribunes with consuls vied
In boldly thrusting public right aside.
Next fell corruption filled the State of Rome;
The fasces sold and sealed the nation's **doom**;
Elections grew an auction of disgrace,
And public life the course for bribery's **race**.
Last usury came, the failing debtor sued,
And desperate need was ripe for civil blood.

Phars. IX. 189-213.

CATO ON THE DEATH OF POMPEY.

A MAN, he said, is gone unequal far
   To our good sires in reverence for the law,
Yet useful in an age that knew not right,
One who could power with liberty unite,
Uncrowned 'mid willing subjects could remain,
The Senate rule, yet let the Senate reign.
The conqueror's force he hated to unmask,
And what he might demand he stooped to ask.
If vast his wealth, no bounds his largess knew;
He drew the sword, but he could sheathe it too.
War was his trade, yet he to peace inclined,
Gladly command accepted — and resigned.
His home was virtuous and austere, nor showed
In aught that there thy master, Rome, abode.
He left a name that nations shall revere,
That to a grateful land shall still be dear.
Marius and Sulla genuine freedom slew,
With Pompey e'en the counterfeit withdrew.
Now usurpation will unveil its face,
Nor seek with forms of law its acts to grace.
Thrice happy thou whom life with victory left
And murder only of disgrace bereft.
Of all the lots, when naught remains but breath,
The first is death self-sought, the next is — death.

Life under Cæsar's yoke might have been thine,
O be thy fate, when fortune leaves me, mine.
Of Juba's dagger come as kind a thrust;
Rule, tyrants, if ye will, o'er Cato's dust.

Phars. IX. 543-585.

[Cato, on his last march in Africa, comes to the Temple of Jupiter Ammon and is urged by his companions to consult the oracle, but refuses.]

AT Ammon's portals from the motley East
To hear his oracles the people pressed,
But all to the great Roman's name gave way.
Now with one voice Cato's companions pray
That he will test the Libyan prophet's claim,
And prove the truth of immemorial fame.
And foremost Labienus bids him try
To look beneath the veil of destiny.
"A happy chance," he cries, "thus on our road
Presents the fane where speaks this mighty god.
Here to the Syrtes we may learn the clue,
Here of the coming war gain forecast true.
To whom should Heaven reveal its high decree,
To whom speak truth, Cato, if not to thee?
Thy life hath never swerved from duty's line,
Still hast thou strictly kept the law divine.
Here mayest thou hold with Jove communion high,
Learn Cæsar's doom, thy country's destiny;
Learn whether liberty and law shall reign,
Or all this civil blood has flowed in vain.

At least, since virtue is to thee so dear,
Learn what she is, and seek her pattern here."
Cato's own breast was deity's abode:
Thence came an answer worthy of a god.
"What should I ask? Whether to live a slave
Is better, or to fill a soldier's grave?
What life is worth drawn to its utmost span,
And whether length of days brings bliss to man?
Whether tyrannic force can hurt the good,
Or the brave heart need quail at Fortune's mood?
Whether the pure intent makes righteousness,
Or virtue needs the warrant of success?
All this I know; not Ammon can impart
Force to the truth engraven on my heart.
All men alike, though voiceless be the shrine,
Abide in God and act by will divine.
No revelation Deity requires,
But at our birth all men may know inspires.
Nor is truth buried in this barren sand
And doled to few, but speaks in every land.
What temple, but the earth, the sea, the sky,
And Heaven, and virtuous hearts hath Deity?
As far as eye can range or feet can rove
Jove is in all things, all things are in Jove.
Let wavering souls to oracles attend,
The brave man's course is clear, since sure his end.
The valiant and the coward both must fall,
This when Jove tells me, he has told me all."
  This said, he turned him from the temple gate,
  And left the crowd to pry into its fate.

MARTIAL.

Epigram. I. XIII.

Casta suo gladium cum traderet Arria Pæto —

ON THE DEATH OF ARRIA AND PÆTUS.

[Cæcina Pætus had been ordered by the Emperor Claudius to put an end to his life: when he hesitated, his wife, Arria, showed him the way.]

THE poniard, with her life-blood dyed,
   When Arria to her Pætus gave,
" 'Twere painless, my beloved," she cried,
   " If but my death thy life could save."

Epigram. I. XV.

O mihi post nullos Juli memorande sodales —

THE FLEETING JOYS OF LIFE.

FRIEND of my heart — and none of all the band
   Has to that name older or better right —
Julius, thy sixtieth winter is at hand;
   Far-spent is now life's day, and near the night.

Delay not what thou would'st recall too late;
 That which is past, that only call thine own;
Cares without end and tribulations wait;
 Joy tarrieth not, but scarcely come, is flown.

Then grasp it quickly, firmly to thy heart;
 Though firmly grasped, too oft it slips away;
To talk of living is not wisdom's part;
 To-morrow is too late: live thou to-day!

EPIGRAM. I. XXXIX.

Si quis erit, raros inter numerandus amicos —

THE PERFECT FRIEND.

LIVES there a man whose friendship rare
 With antique friendship may compare;
In learning steeped, both old and new,
Yet unpedantic, simple, true;
Whose soul, ingenuous and upright,
Ne'er formed a wish that shunned the light;
Whose sense is sound? If such there be,
My Decianus, thou art he.

Epigram. I. lxxxix.

Alcime, quem raptum domino crescentibus annis

ON THE DEATH OF A YOUNG AND FAVOURITE SLAVE.

DEAR youth, too early lost, who now art laid
    Beneath the turf in green Labicum's glade,
O'er thee no storied urn, no laboured bust
I rear to crumble with the crumbling dust;
But tapering box and shadowy vine shall wave,
And grass, with tears bedewed, shall clothe thy grave.
These gifts my sorrowing love to thee shall bring,
Gifts ever fresh and deathless as the Spring.
O when to me the fatal hour shall come,
Mine be as lowly and as green a tomb!

Epigram. I. xciii.

Fabricio junctus fido requiescit Aquinus—

ON TWO OLD ROMAN OFFICERS BURIED SIDE BY SIDE.

[A pleasant trait of Roman military life.]

AQUINUS here by his Fabricius lies,
    Glad that he first was summoned to the skies:
The equal honours of each martial chief
Their tombs set forth. This record is more brief—
Comrades they were in virtue to the end,
And each, rare glory! earned the name of friend.

Epigram. II. xi.

Quod fronte Selium nubila vides, Rufe —

THE DINER-OUT DISAPPOINTED.

BEHOLD, on Selius' brow, how dark the shade;
   How late he roams beneath the colonnade;
How his grim face betrays some secret wound;
How with his nose he almost scrapes the ground.
He beats his breast, he rends his hair. What now?
Has Selius lost a friend, or brother? No!
His brace of sons still live, long be their life!
Safe are his slaves, his chattels, and his wife;
His steward's, his bailiff's books are right — what doom
So dire has fallen on him? He dines at home!

Epigram. II. lxviii.

Quod te nomine jam tuo saluto —

A REVOLT.

THINK not I have become a boor
   If I " My Lord " thee now no more,
My haughty friend. I've paid my fee —
All I was worth — for liberty.
Who wants what lords to servants give
A lord must own, a servant live.
But, my good Olus, take my word,
Who needs no servant wants no lord.

Epigram. III. xxi.

Proscriptum famulus servavit fronte notatus —

[On a slave who, having been branded by a cruel master, afterwards saved that master's life from massacre under proscription. A welcome tribute from the Roman Poet to humanity.]

WHEN, scarred with cruel brand, the slave
    Snatched from the murderer's hand
His proscript lord, not life he gave
    His tyrant, but the brand.

Epigram. III. xxxv.

Artis Phidiacæ toreuma clarum —

Epigram. III. xli.

Inserta phialæ Mentoris manu ducta —

ON TWO WORKS OF ART.

[Showing the extreme value which the Ancients set on exact imitation.]

THESE fishes Phidias wrought: with life by him
    They are endowed; add water and they swim.

THAT lizard on the goblet makes thee start.
    Fear not; it lives only by Mentor's art.

Epigram. III. LVIII.

Baiana nostri villa, Basse, Faustini —

[This piece gives a pleasant picture of Roman country life, and shows that there was something left under the Empire better than the vast estates tilled by slave gangs, which Pliny calls the ruin of Italy.]

FAUSTINUS is a man of taste;
    Yet is his Baian seat no waste
Of useless myrtle, barren plane,
Clipped box, like many a grand domain
That covers miles with empty state:
But country unsophisticate.
In every corner grain is crammed,
Casks fragrant of old wine are jammed.
Here, at the turning of the year,
Vinedressers house the vintage sere.
Grim bulls in grassy valleys low
And the calf butts with hornless brow.
Poultry of every clime and sort
Ramble in dirt about the court,
The screaming geese, flamingoes red,
Peacocks with jewelled tail outspread,
Pied partridges, pheasants that come
From Colchian strand, dark magic's home,
And Afric's birds of many spots.
The cock amidst his harem struts
While on the tower aloft doves coo
And pigeons flap and turtles woo.

Pigs to the good wife's apron scurry,
Lambs to their milky mothers hurry.
The fire, well-heaped, burns bright and high,
Around it crowds the nursery.
No butler here from lack of toil
Grows sick, no trainer wastes his oil,
Lounging at ease; but forth they fare
The fish with quivering line to snare,
The crafty springe for birds to set,
Or catch the deer with circling net.
Pleased with the garden's easy work
The city hands take spade and fork;
The curly-headed striplings ask
The bailiff for a merry task
Without their pedagogue's command;
E'en the sleek eunuch bears a hand.
Then country callers, many a one,
Troop in, and empty-handed none;
This brings a honeycomb, that a pail
Of milk from green Sassinum's dale;
Capons or dormice plump another,
Or kid, reft from his shaggy mother.
Basket on arm, stout lasses come
With gifts from many a thrifty home.
Work over, each, a willing guest,
Is bidden to no niggard feast,
Where all may revel at their will,
And servants eat, like guests, their fill.
But thou, friend Bassus, close to town,
On trim starvation lookest down,

Seest laurels, laurels everywhere;
No need the thief from fruit to scare.
Town bread thy vinedresser must eat;
The town sends greens, eggs, cheese, and meat.
Such country is — my friend must own —
Not country, but town out of town.

Epigram. IV. VIII.

Prima salutantes atque altera continet hora—

THE OCCUPATION OF A ROMAN DAY.

VISITS consume the first, the second hour;
   When comes the third, hoarse pleaders show
     their power;
At four to business Rome herself betakes;
At six she goes to sleep, by seven she wakes;
By nine well breathed from exercise we rest,
And in the banquet hall the couch is pressed.
Now, when thy skill, greatest of cooks, has spread
The ambrosial feast, let Martial's rhymes be read,
With mighty hand while Cæsar holds the bowl,
When draughts of nectar have relaxed his soul.
Now trifles pass. My giddy Muse would fear
Jove to approach in morning mood severe.

Epigram. IV. xiii.

Claudia, Rufe, meo nubit Peregrina Pudenti —

ON A FRIEND'S WEDDING.

MY Pudens shall his Claudia wed this day.
   Shed, torch of Hymen, shed thy brightest ray!
So costly nard and cinnamon combine,
So blends sweet honey with the luscious wine.
So clasps the tender vine her elm, so love
The lotus leaves the stream, myrtles the cove.
Fair Concord, dwell for ever by that bed;
Let Venus bless the pair so meetly wed;
May the wife love with love that grows not cold,
And never to her husband's eye seem old.

Epigram. V. xx.

Si tecum mihi, care Martialis —

THE TRUE BUSINESS OF LIFE.

O COULD both thou and I, my friend,
   From care and trouble freed,
Our quiet days at pleasure spend
   And taste of life indeed,

We'd bid farewell to marble halls,
   The sad abodes of state,
To law, with all its dismal brawls,
   To trappings of the great;

We'd seek the book, the cheerful talk,
   At noonday in the shade,
The bath, the ride, the pleasant walk
   In the cool colonnade.

Dead to our better selves we see
   The golden hours take flight,
Still scored against us as they flee;
   Then haste to live aright.

Epigram. V. XLII.

Callidus effracta nummos fur auferet arca —

AN EXHORTATION TO LIBERALITY.

THE crafty thief your cash-box may invade;
   Your father's house in ashes may be laid;
Your steward be swindled by a harlot's guile;
Your merchandise become the ocean's spoil.
Your debtor may a bankrupt prove; your field,
The sower's hopes belied, no harvest yield;
What thou hast given to friends, and that alone,
Defies misfortune, and is still thy own.

Epigram. VIII. xviii.

Si tua, Cirini, promas epigrammata vulgo —

LITERARY CHIVALRY.

GIVEN to the world, those epigrams of thine,
   My friend Cirinius, might have rivalled mine;
But thou hast such regard for friendship shown
As to prefer my glory to thy own.
So, Virgil, though he might with Pindar's strain
Have vied, to Horace left his own domain.
To Varius so he left the Roman stage,
Himself the born tragedian of the age.
Money or lands to give is nothing new,
They who make presents of renown are few.

Epigram. VIII. lxix.

Miraris veteres, Vacerra, solos —

THE REVERSE OF THE LAST.

VACERRA lauds no living poet's lays,
   But for departed genius keeps his praise.
I, alas, live, nor deem it worth my while
To die, that I may win Vacerra's smile.

Epigram. X. xxiv.

Natales mihi Martiæ Calendæ —

ON HIS OWN BIRTHDAY, MARCH 1.

[To explain lines three and four, it should be said that girls usually received presents while men sent them on the first of March, but Martial, the day being his birthday, received presents from female as well as male friends.]

ABOVE all days bright is my natal morn.
Blest I who, March, upon thy Kalends born,
Receive from ladies presents many a one,
While others get them from the men alone.
Fifty and seven times at the altar now
Martial has duly paid his birthday vow.
Grant, if it be your pleasure, powers divine
That I to fifty-seven may add twice nine,
And thus, when life's three stages I have past,
Yet sound and brisk and hearty to the last
To Proserpine's domain may wend my way.
Of Nestor's age I ask not one more day.

Epigram. X. xlvii.

Vitam quæ faciunt beatiorem —

A ROMAN GENTLEMAN'S IDEA OF HAPPINESS.

WHAT makes a happy life, dear friend,
If thou would'st briefly learn, attend.
An income left, not earned by toil;

Some acres of a kindly soil;
The pot unfailing on the fire;
No lawsuits; seldom town attire;
Health; strength with grace; a peaceful mind;
Shrewdness with honesty combined;
Plain living; equal friends and free;
Evenings of temperate gaiety;
A wife discreet, yet blithe and bright;
Sound slumber, that lends wings to night.
With all thy heart embrace thy lot,
Wish not for death and fear it not.

Epigram. X. L.

Frangat Idumæas tristris Victoria palmas—

ON THE UNTIMELY DEATH OF A FAMOUS CHARIOTEER.

LET Victory, sorrowing, cast her palm away,
   Let Favour beat her breast and wail the day,
Let Honour don the mourner's dark attire,
And Glory fling her wreath upon the pyre.
Snatched in his prime, Scorpus, sad thought! must go
To yoke night's horses in the realm below.
Swift flew the chariot, soon the goal was won;
Another race thou hast too quickly run.

Epigram. XII. xxxiv.

Triginta mihi quatuorque messes —

VICISSITUDES OF FRIENDSHIP.

MY friend, since thou and I first met,
    This is the thirty-fourth December;
Some things there are we'd fain forget,
    More that 'tis pleasant to remember.

Let for each pain a black ball stand,
    For every pleasure past a white one,
And thou wilt find, when all are scanned,
    The major part will be the bright one.

He who would heartache never know,
    He who unruffled calmness treasures,
Must friendship's chequered bliss forego;
    Who has no pain has fewer pleasures.

CLAUDIAN.

In Rufinum, I. 1–21.

Sæpe mihi dubiam traxit sententia mentem —

[The successful career of the infamous favourite Rufinus had shaken Claudian's faith in Providence. By the fall of Rufinus the poet's faith is restored.]

OFTTIMES had doubt distraught my mind.
    Did Heaven look down on human kind,
Or was the Guiding Power a dream,
And chance o'er men's affairs supreme?
When I surveyed great Nature's law,
The ordered tides and seasons saw,
Day following night, night following day,
All seemed to own an Author's sway,
Whose fiat ruled the starry choir,
Who robed the glorious sun with fire,
Bade the moon shine with borrowed light
And earth yield all her fruits aright,
Poised the round world and taught the wave
Within its bounding shore to rave.
But when I turned to man's estate
And saw how dark the ways of fate,

Saw vice victorious mounting high,
And suffering worth neglected lie,
Doubt triumphed and my faith grew cold.
Sadly I turned to those who hold
That all is born of atoms blind,
Whirled through the void, without a mind,
And that the gods, if gods there be,
Are careless of humanity.
But now my soul her faith regains,
Rufinus falls, Heaven's justice reigns :
The bad are raised only to show
Heaven's justice in their overthrow.

WORKS BY THE SAME AUTHOR.

CANADA AND THE CANADIAN QUESTION.

With Map. 8vo, $2.00.

"This is a timely book, but it is something more. . . . It is as valuable for its discriminating comments upon contemporary social life in Canada, as for its brilliant review of Canada's political history, and its convincing arguments in favor of her commercial union with the United States. . . . Mr. Smith is a wonderfully acute critic." — *Christian Union.*

"These questions — for, as will be seen, there are many comprised under one head — are all treated in Professor Smith's latest volume with the clearness and force which belong to all his writings." — *Critic.*

"The book is admirably concise in method, often epigrammatic in the sweeping generalizations. The method is modern, moreover, in that it takes account of social forms and prejudices, of popular thought, in short, as well as of the political plans of the few so-called leaders of men." — *Hamlin Garland,* in *The Arena.*

THREE ENGLISH STATESMEN.

A Course of Lectures on the Political History of England. 12mo, $1.50.

THE CONDUCT OF ENGLAND TO IRELAND.

An Address. 8vo, paper, 15 cents.

A TRIP TO ENGLAND.

18mo, cloth, gilt, 75 cents.

"A delightful little work, telling in a most charming, rambling, yet systematic way what is to be seen of interest in England." — *Chicago Times.*

"So delightful a cicerone as Mr. Goldwin Smith proves himself in 'A Trip to England' does not often fall to the lot of the non-personally conducted. . . . Meissonnier-like in its diminutiveness, but also Meissonnier-like in its mastery." — *Critic.*

MACMILLAN & CO., PUBLISHERS,
NEW YORK.

THE WORKS OF MR. WILLIAM WINTER.

Just Published.

Shadows of the Stage.
Second Series.

18mo, cloth, gilt top, 75 cents.

⁎ Also a limited edition, printed on laid paper, with ample margins, $2.00.

Shakespeare's England.
18mo, cloth, gilt top, 75 cents.

Gray Days and Gold.
18mo, cloth, gilt top, 75 cents.

Old Shrines and Ivy.
18mo, cloth, gilt top, 75 cents.

Shadows of the Stage.
First Series.

18mo, cloth, gilt top, 75 cents.

The above four volumes, uniformly bound in half calf or half morocco, in a box, $8.00.

⁎ Also a limited edition, printed on laid paper, with ample margins, four volumes, in a box, $8.00.

Wanderers.

Being a Collection of the Poems of WILLIAM WINTER. New Edition, Revised and Enlarged. With a Portrait of the Author. 18mo, cloth, gilt top, 75 cents.

⁎ Also a limited large-paper edition, printed on English hand-made paper. Price $2.50.

George William Curtis. WITH PORTRAIT.
18mo, cloth, gilt top, 75 cents.

In the Press.

The Life and Art of Edwin Booth.
12mo, cloth.

⁎ Also a limited edition on large paper, with proof illustrations.

www.ingramcontent.com/pod-product-compliance
Lightning Source LLC
Chambersburg PA
CBHW020155170426
43199CB00010B/1053